Bless This Food

Photographed and hand painted by Kathleen Francour

Stories by Sylvia Seymour

Photography © 2002 Kathleen Francour
Carefree, Arizona. All rights reserved.

Louis Weber, C.E.O.
Publications International, Ltd.
7373 North Cicero Avenue
Lincolnwood, Illinois 60712

www.pubint.com

ISBN: 0-7853-7050-1

Jesus Loves
the
Little Children
™

Our Garden

The Rogers family was eating food from their garden for supper. Gregory was proud of the golden ears of corn that he helped grow. Richard beamed as Mother placed the potatoes he grew on the table. Jane's onions were in the salad with Mom's cucumbers and Dad's tomatoes.

"These are MY potatoes and I want them all," Richard announced as he pulled them over to his plate.

"Well, then you can't have any of MY corn," said Gregory.

"Are you forgetting who made all the vegetables?" asked Mother.

"We did!"

"God MADE them and we just took care of the garden. Now let's all share and thank Jesus for the food He has given us."

Each time we eat,
may we remember God's love.

God bless us, every one!

Charles Dickens

While they were eating,
Jesus took bread, gave thanks and broke it.

Matthew 26:26

O you who feeds the little bird,
bless our food, O Lord.

Let us in peace eat the food
that God has provided for us.
Praise be to God for all His gifts.

Amen.

O God, make us able
for all that's on the table!

Amen.

Thank You, Jesus

Dad usually said the blessing at breakfast, but this morning he asked everyone to share something they were thankful for. They all bowed their heads.

"Thank you, Jesus, for our food," said Colleen.

"Thank you for Mommy and Daddy," said Terry.

"Thank you, Jesus, for my friends," said Tony.

Mom and Dad prayed, too. Then it was Maria's turn to pray. Maria was the youngest. "What could she thank Jesus for?" she thought. "Jesus, thank you for…, for…, for EVERYONE!"

The family burst into laughter.

"AMEN," they all said together. "Now, let's eat!"

O Lord God, heavenly Father,
bless us and these thy gifts,
which we shall accept from
Thy tender goodness.
Feed our souls with Your wisdom
so that we may partake
in Your heavenly table as well,
Lord Jesus Christ.

Amen.

Bless, O Lord, Your gifts to our use
and us to Your service, for Christ's sake.

Amen.

Give thanks to the Lord…who gives food
to every creature.

Psalm 136:1,25

Be present at our table, Lord.
    Be here and everywhere adored.
His mercies bless and grant that we
    May strengthened for Thy service be.
Amen.

Two Spoons

"Mommy, may Sarah eat with us tonight? Her mom is working late. Please, Mommy, please!" begged Michelle.

Mother looked at little Sarah. She looked so lonely. "Yes, Sarah may stay."

The dinner was delicious. Michelle helped her mother clear the table for dessert. They were having her favorite dessert, chocolate pudding. Suddenly Michelle realized that there wasn't a bowl for Sarah. What should she do? She gave the last bowl to her best friend.

Sarah saw that Michelle did not have any pudding. "Oh, Michelle," she said. "This is too much pudding for me. Can we share?"

Michelle's face lit up with joy. "Yes, Sarah. I'll get two spoons."

We thank Thee, Lord,
   For happy hearts,
For rain and sunny weather;
   We thank Thee, Lord,
For this our food,
   And that we are together.

God is great,
   God is good,
And we thank Him
   For our food.

Thank you for the world so sweet,
Thank you for the food we eat.
Thank you for the birds that sing,
Thank you, God, for everything.

For every cup and plateful,
God make us truly grateful!

Each time we eat,
may we remember
God's love.
Amen.

Thank you, O Lord,
for these, Thy gifts
which we are about to receive
from Thy bounty.

Amen.